Saxophone

Note Speller

M000034013

by FRED WEBER

A SYSTEMATIZED SET OF WORK SHEETS
FOR SUPPLEMENTING ANY ELEMENTARY CLASS OR PRIVATE METHOD.

DESIGNED TO HELP THE STUDENT GAIN A BETTER UNDERSTANDING OF THE PROBLEMS
OF FINGERING AND READING MUSIC AND AT THE SAME TIME SAVE VALUABLE LESSON TIME.

Published for:
Flute and Piccolo (EL00462)
Clarinet (EL00448)
Oboe (EL00463)
Bassoon (EL00464)
Saxophone (EL00451)

Trumpet (Baritone T.C.) (EL00449)
French Horn (EL00465)
Trombone (EL00450)
Baritone B.C. (EL00467)
Tuba (EL00468)
Drum Rhythm Speller (EL01063)

Diagram of the Instrument
Showing location of finger-plates and keys.

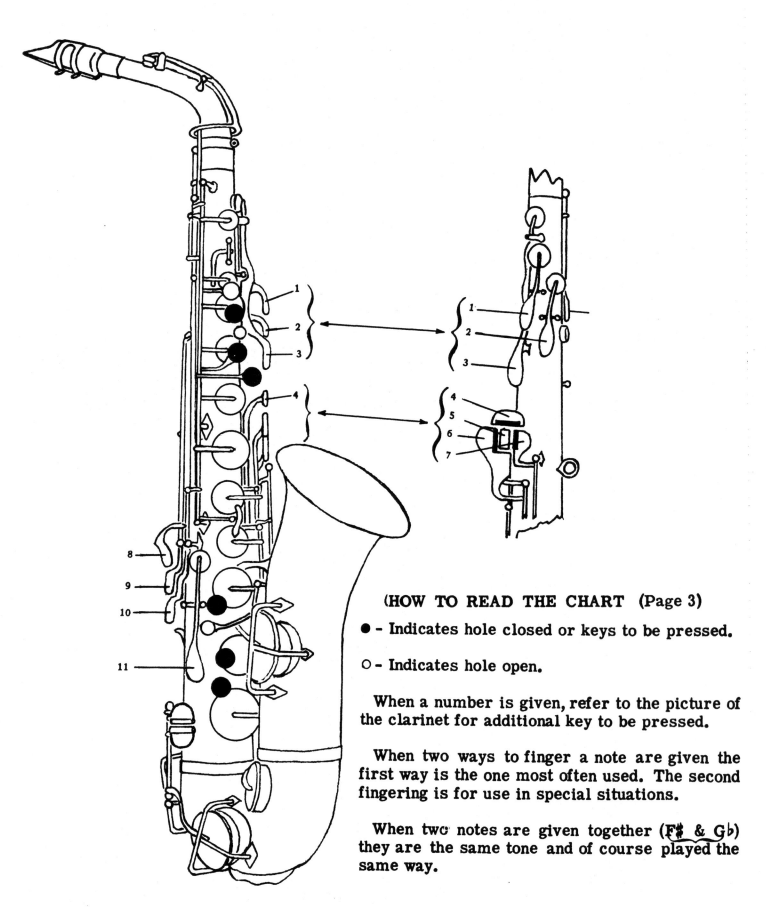

(HOW TO READ THE CHART (Page 3)

● - Indicates hole closed or keys to be pressed.

○ - Indicates hole open.

When a number is given, refer to the picture of the clarinet for additional key to be pressed.

When two ways to finger a note are given the first way is the one most often used. The second fingering is for use in special situations.

When two notes are given together (F# & Gb) they are the same tone and of course played the same way.

Elementary Fingering Chart

In order to make the fingering chart as easy to understand as possible, only those fingerings necessary in the elementary phase of saxophone playing, are given.

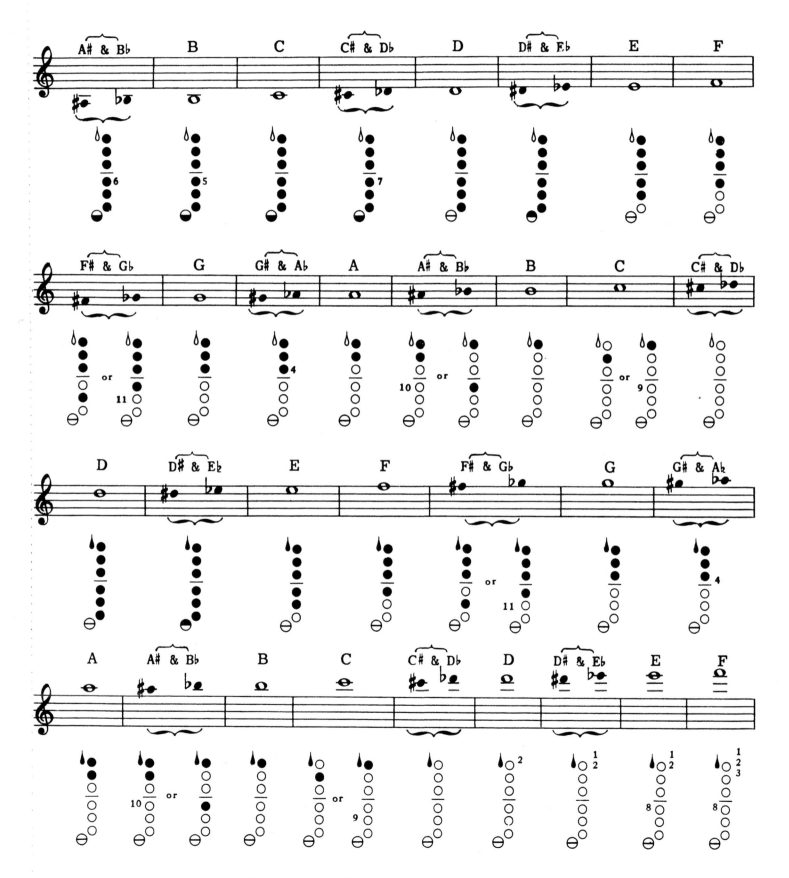

LESSON 1

You should know the following.

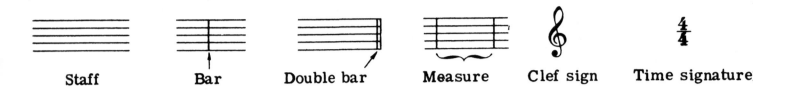

Staff   Bar   Double bar   Measure   Clef sign   Time signature

1 Match the symbols in the **TOP** line with their names.
The first one is done for you.

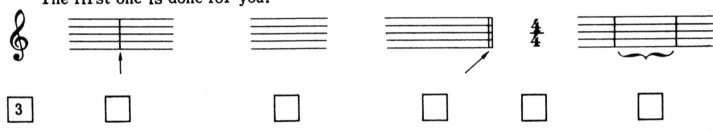

1-Staff; 2-Measure; 3-Clef sign; 4-Bar; 5-Time signature; 6-Double bar.

2 The Treble Clef sign () is usually found at the beginning of each staff of clarinet music.
There are 3 easy steps in learning to draw this sign.

a - Step 1-A straight
line extending above
and below the staff.

Step 2-A curved line
that crosses the up
and down line on the
4th line of the staff.

Step 3-A curved line
touching the bottom
line and the 3rd line
as above.

b - Draw 3 lines as in
step one above.

Draw the 3 curved lines
as in step 2 above.

Complete the curve as
in step 3 above.

Draw 3 complete Treble
Clef signs.

LESSON 2

1 a - Put names of notes in squares above staff.
     b - Mark the fingering.

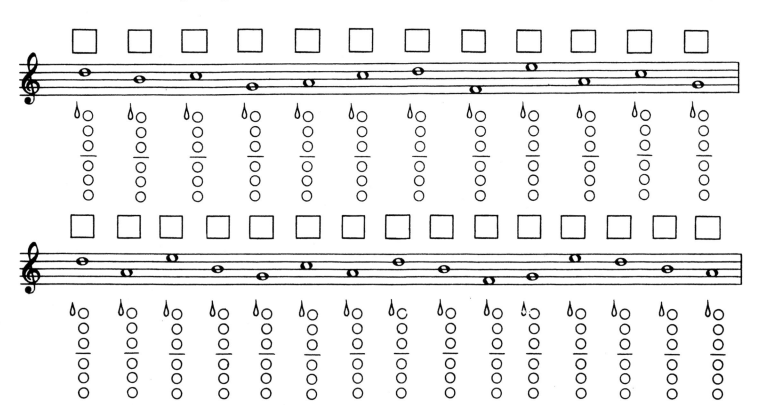

2 Put the number of the line or space the note is on, in the square and write below whether the note is on a line or space.

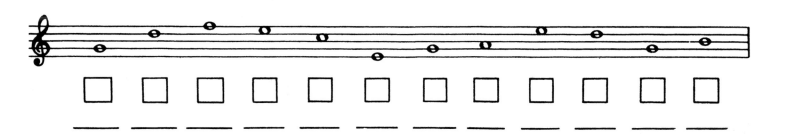

LESSON 3

1 a - Put notes called for on the staff. (Use notes you have learned).
b - Mark fingerings.

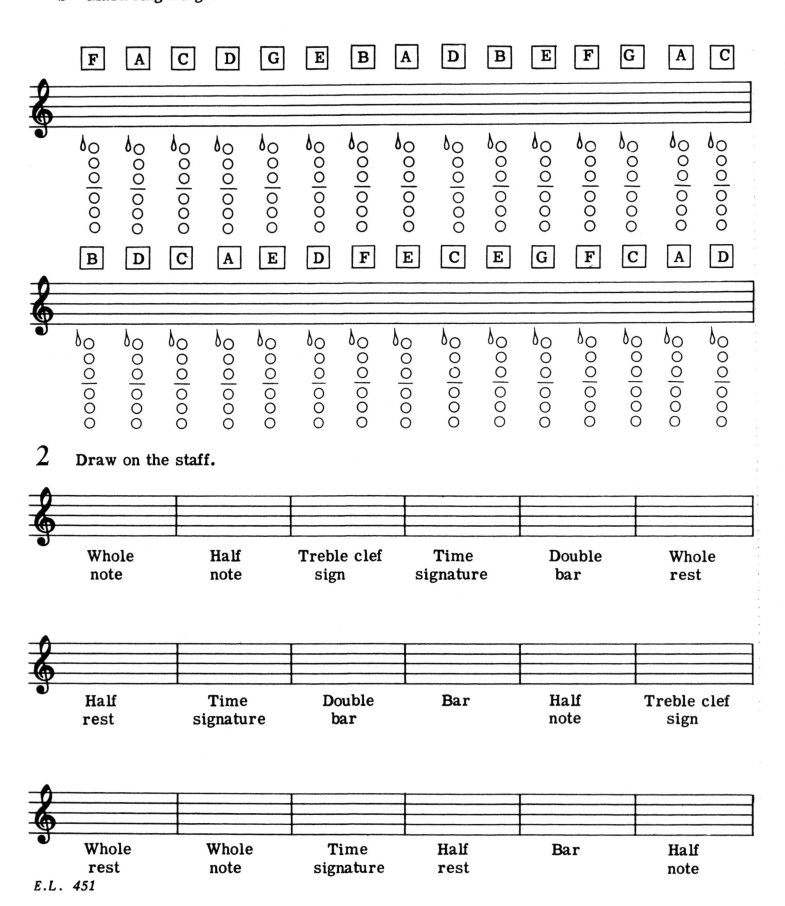

2 Draw on the staff.

| Whole note | Half note | Treble clef sign | Time signature | Double bar | Whole rest |

| Half rest | Time signature | Double bar | Bar | Half note | Treble clef sign |

| Whole rest | Whole note | Time signature | Half rest | Bar | Half note |

LESSON 4

1 a - Write notes on the staff as indicated by fingering.
b - Name the notes.

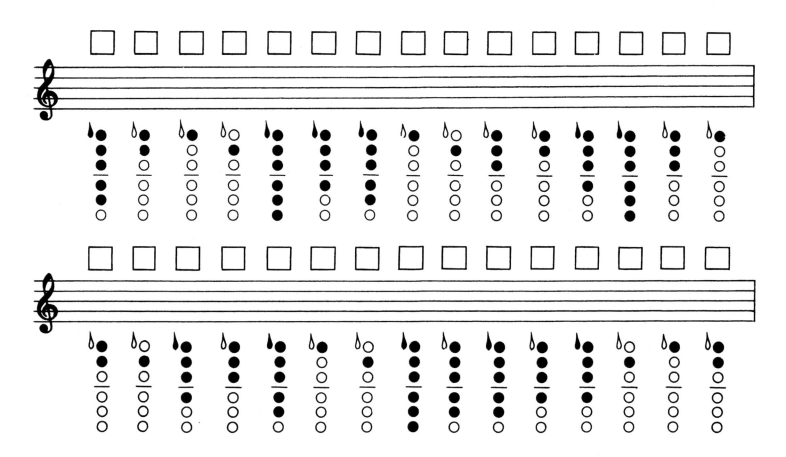

2 a - Put notes on the lines and spaces as called for.
b - Put names of notes in the boxes.

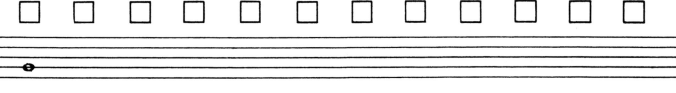

2	3	1	4	2	3	4	4	1	5	2	3
line	space	line	line	space	space	line	space	space	line	space	line

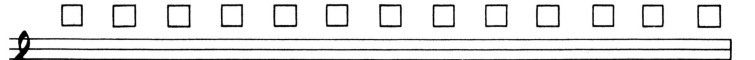

3	5	4	3	1	4	2	2	4	4	5	1	3
space	line	space	space	line	line	line	space	space	line	line	space	space

LESSON 5

1 a - Name the notes.
   b - Mark fingerings. (See picture, page 2, for numbers of additional keys
       when needed.)

*See note.

*Note - See picture, page 2, for number of additional keys if necessary.

2 What are the names of notes on the following lines and spaces?

1 - 1st line -[E]	11 - 4th line - ☐
2 - 2nd space - ☐	12 - 3rd line - ☐
3 - 5th line - ☐	13 - 1st line - ☐
4 - 4th space - ☐	14 - 1st space - ☐
5 - 3rd line - ☐	15 - 5th line - ☐
6 - 2nd line - ☐	16 - 1st space - ☐
7 - 3rd space - ☐	17 - 2nd space - ☐
8 - 5th line - ☐	18 - 2nd line - ☐
9 - 4th space - ☐	19 - 3rd line - ☐
10-2nd line - ☐	20 - 4th space - ☐

E.L. 451

LESSON 6

1 a - Put notes called for on the staff.
  b - Mark fingerings.

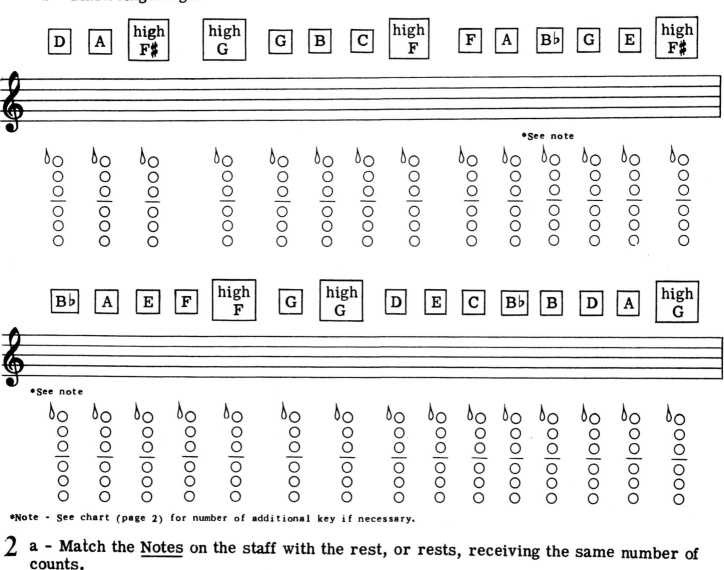

*Note - See chart (page 2) for number of additional key if necessary.

2 a - Match the <u>Notes</u> on the staff with the rest, or rests, receiving the same number of counts.

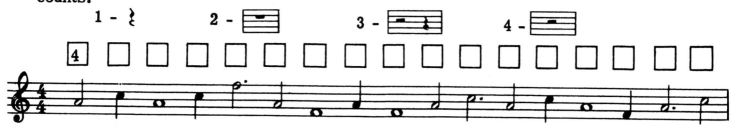

b - Match the <u>Rests</u> on the staff with the note receiving the same number of counts. (In 4/4 time).

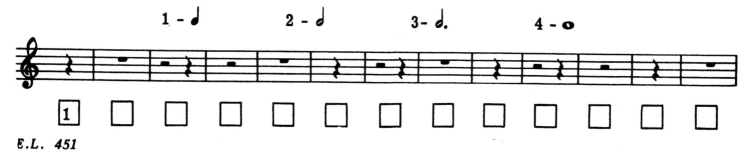

10

LESSON 7

1 Match the Symbols on the staff with their names.
The first one is done for you.

1 - Sharp	5 - Clef Sign	9 - Half note
2 - Tie	6 - Whole note	10- Flat
3 - Bar	7 - Quarter rest	11- Quarter note
4 - Time Signature	8 - Natural sign	12- Half rest
		13- Whole rest

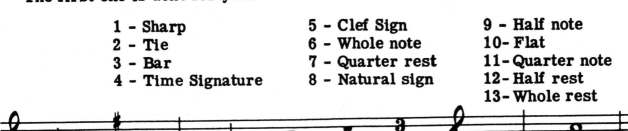

2 Give the number of counts the notes and rests receive in 4/4 time.

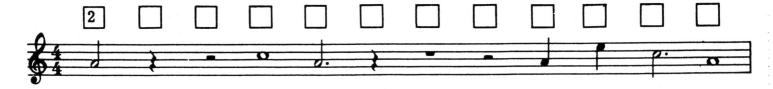

3 Write the counting in the measures below. The first measure is done for you.
Always remember to think the number of the count when playing.

1 2 3 4

LESSON 8

1 a - Name the notes.
b - Mark fingering.

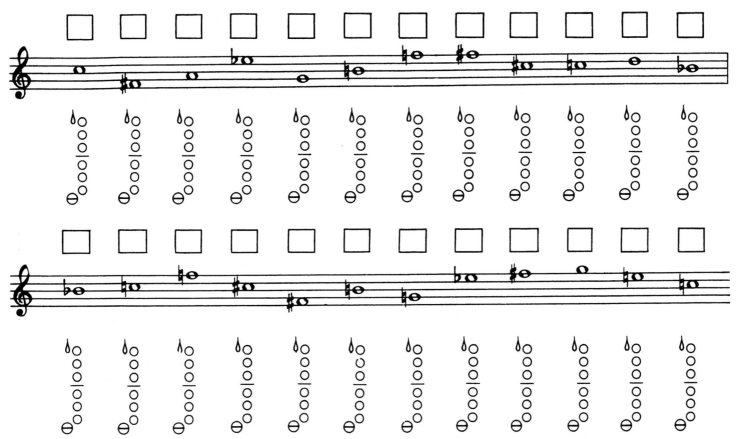

2 A Tie combines 2 or more notes on the same line or space.
A Slur is a curved line that looks like a tie but it joins groups of notes on different lines and spaces.
Mark the ties below with a T and slurs with an S.

LESSON 9

1 The following notes spell words. What are they?

2 Write the following words on the staff.
Where you have learned two notes with the same name - write the lowest one.

F A D E   B A D G E   C A F E   D A D   A B E   D E A D   C A B

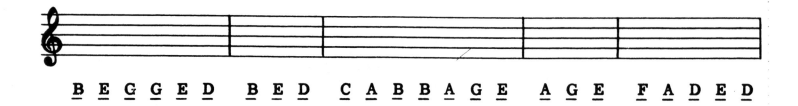

B E G G E D   B E D   C A B B A G E   A G E   F A D E D

3 Write the counting under the following measures.

1 2 3 4

LESSON 10

1 a - Put the notes called for on the staff.
b - Mark fingerings. (See page 2 for numbers of additional keys if necessary).

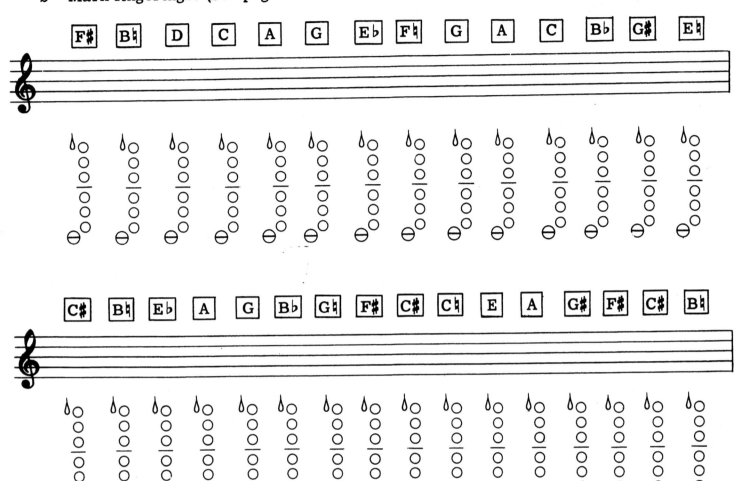

2 Write **T** under the notes that should be tongued and **S** under those that should be slurred. Tongue only the first note of each slur.

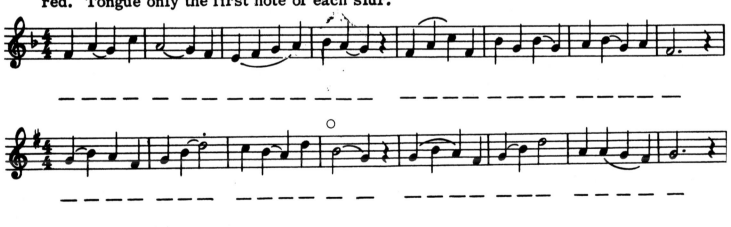

3 Write the note receiving the number of counts called for in 4/4 time.

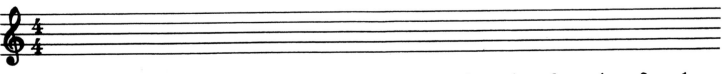

LESSON 11

1 a - The fingerings below are given. Write the notes they produce.
b - Name the notes.

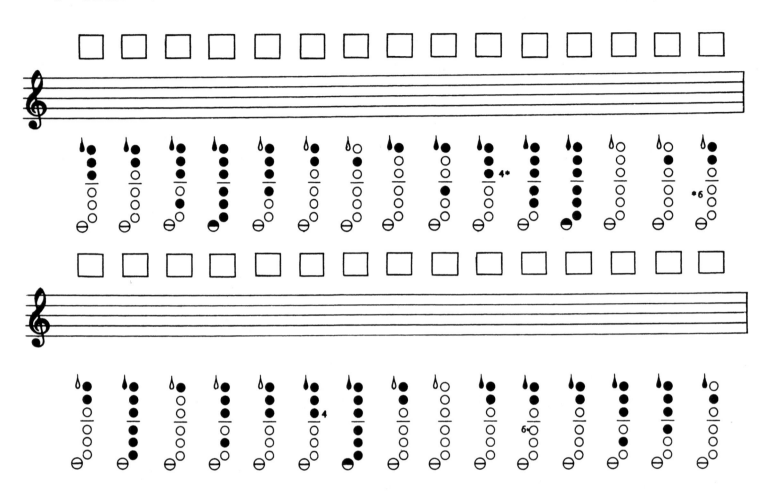

*See picture of Sax. page 2.

2 Three of the most common kinds of time are 4/4; 3/4; & 2/4.
4/4 means there are 4 counts in each measure.
3/4 means there are 3 counts in each measure.
2/4 means there are 3 counts in each measure.
Put the correct time signature at the beginning of each measure.

3 Write the counting under the measures below.

1 2 3 4

LESSON 12

1 a - Name the notes.
b - Mark the fingering.

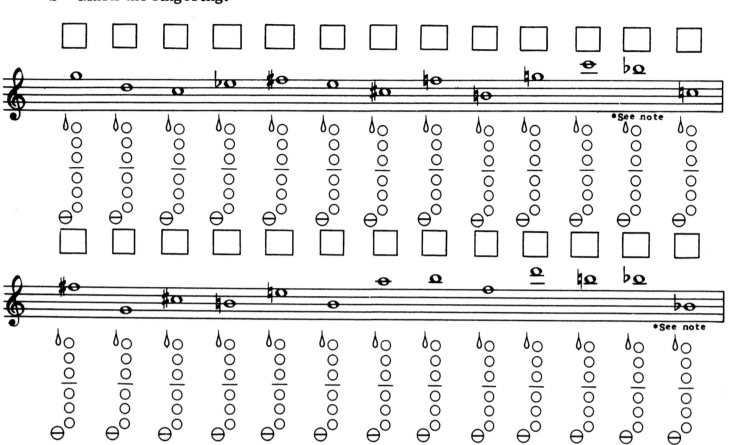

*Note - See picture (page 2) for number of additional key

2 Add the time received by the notes, in 4/4 time, and put the total in the square.

o + ♩ + ♩ = ☐   o + ♩. + o = ☐

♩ + ♩. + ♩ = ☐   ♩. + ♩ + ♩ = ☐

o + ♩ + ♩ = ☐   ♩ + ♩ + ♩. = ☐

♩ + o + ♩. = ☐   ♩ + ♩ + ♩. = ☐

♩ + ♩ + ♩ = ☐   ♩ + o + ♩ = ☐

3 Match the following.

D . C.   - ☐   1 - The end

Fine   - ☐   2 - Repeat

𝄂𝄀   - ☐   3 - Go back to the beginning

𝄐   - ☐   4 - 4/4 time

C   - ☐   5 - Give extra time (hold).

*Name of Student*_____

1 a – Write the notes on the staff. (Use higher octave).
b – Mark fingering.

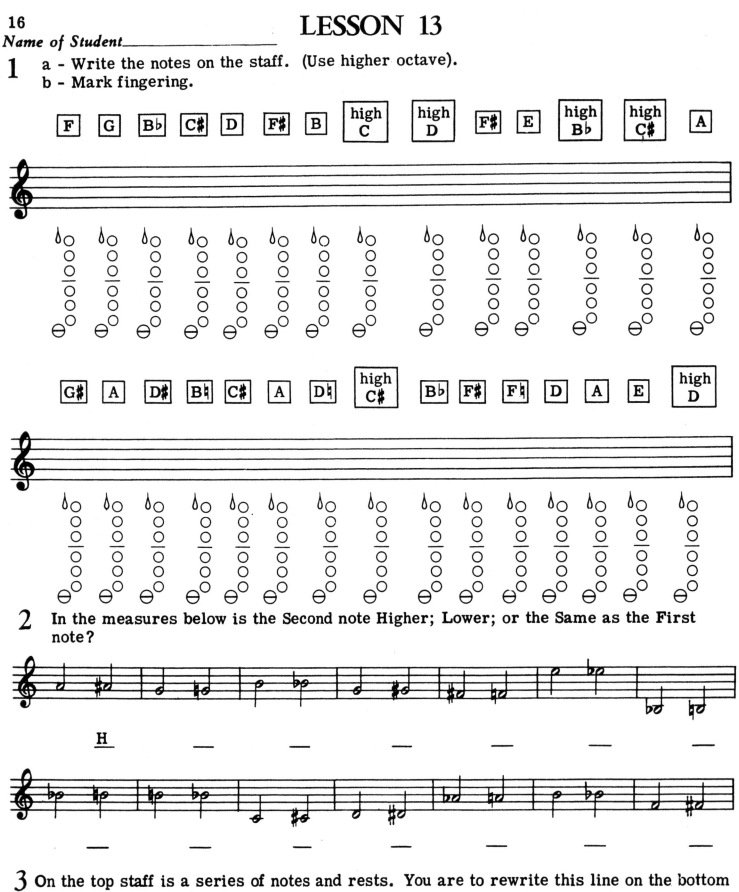

2 In the measures below is the Second note Higher; Lower; or the Same as the First note?

H _____ _____ _____ _____ _____ _____

_____ _____ _____ _____

3 On the top staff is a series of notes and rests. You are to rewrite this line on the bottom staff changing notes to rests of the same time value and rests to notes of the same time value.

sample   etc.

LESSON 14

1 a – Name the notes.
b – Mark fingering. (See page 2 for numbers of additional keys when necessary).

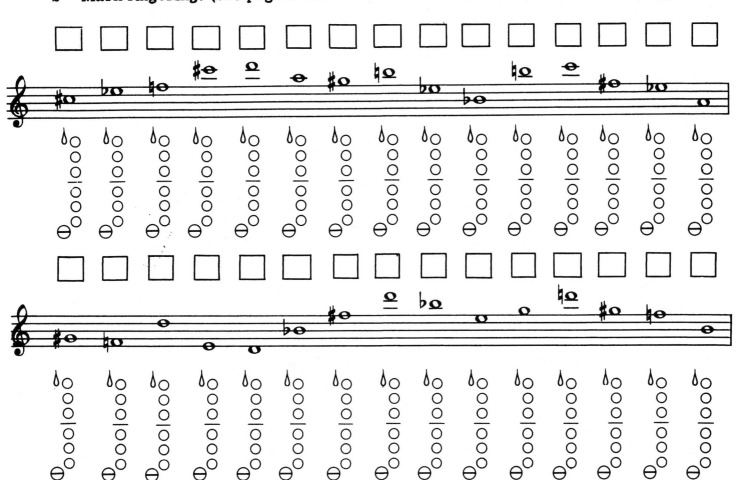

2 a – Write the letter name of the Sharps. (A Sharp is on the line or space that passes through the center (♯) of the Sharp.)

A♯ _ _ _ _ _ _ _ _ _ _ _ _

b – Write the letter name of the Flats. (A Flat is on the line or space that passes through the center (♭) of the Flat.

_ _ _ _ _ _ _ _ _ _ _ _ _ _

3 Write the counting under the measures below.

1 2 3   4

LESSON 15

1 a - Write the full names of the notes.
b - Mark the fingerings.

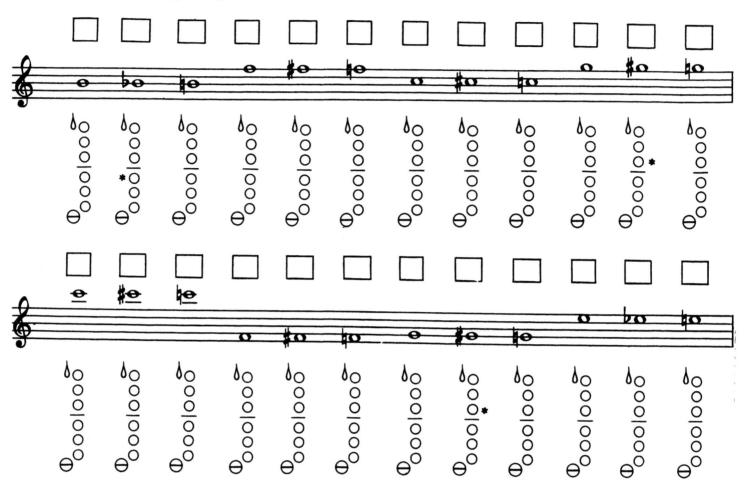

*See picture (page 2) for number of additional key.

2 a - Put in the Bar lines. (Note Time signatures).
b - Write the counting under each measure.

LESSON 16

1 A flat or sharp remains in effect througnout the entire measure unless cancelled by a natural (♮).

In the examples below-is the Third note like the First, Second or Both?

2nd ___ ___ ___ ___

___ ___ ___ ___

2 Put the following on the staff below:

1 - Sharp
2 - Half note
3 - Clef sign
4 - Time signature
5 - Quarter rest

6 - Natural sign
7 - Flat
8 - Whole rest
9 - Half rest
10-Dotted half note

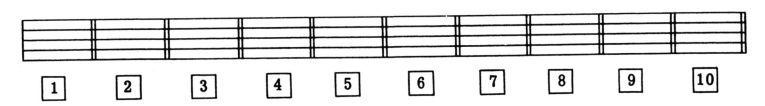

| 1 | 2 | 3 | 4 | 5 | 6 | 7 | 8 | 9 | 10 |

3 Write on the staff.

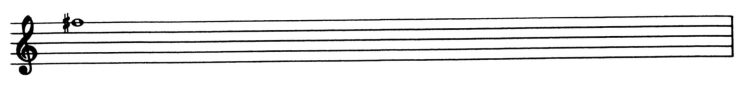

F♯   E♮   C♯   B♭   F♮   E♭   C♮   B♮   D♯   G♯   A♭   D♭

E.L. 451

LESSON 17

1 The fingerings are given.
  a – Put the note on the staff.
  b – Name the note.

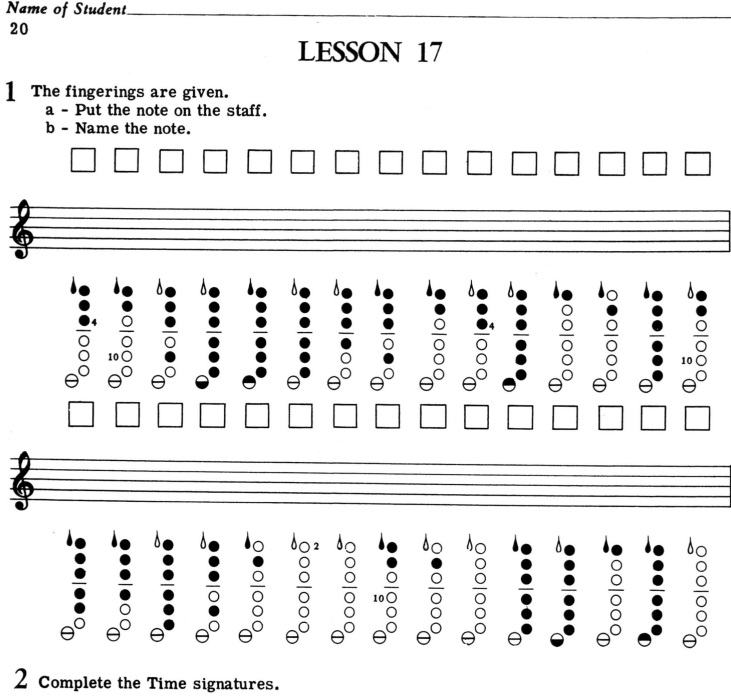

2 Complete the Time signatures.

3 Put in Bar lines and write counting under each measure.

LESSON 18

1 Add the time of the notes and rests in 4/4 time.

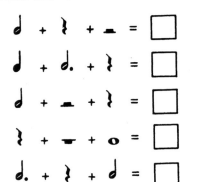

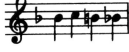   

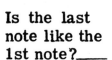   

2 Answer Yes or No to the questions below.

Is the last note like the 1st note?____

Is the last note like the 2nd note?____

Is the last note like the 3rd note?____

Is the last note like the 1st note?____

Is the last note like the 1st note?____

Is the last note like the 1st note?____

Is the last note like the 1st note?____

Is the last note like the 1st note?____

Is the last note like the 1st note?____

Is the last note like the 1st note?____

3 a – Put in Bar lines. (Note Time signatures).
b – Write **T** under the notes that should be tongued and **S** under those that are not tongued.

LESSON 19

1 a - Name the notes (full name).
   b - Mark fingering.

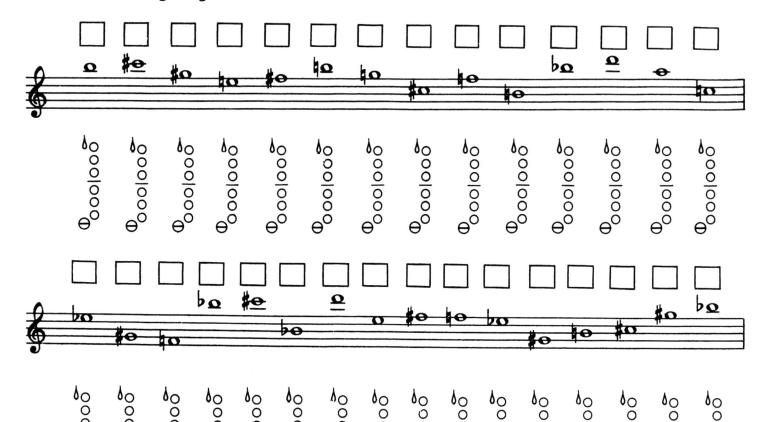

2 Circle the notes affected by the key signatures. When we have one sharp in the key signatures it is always F♯.

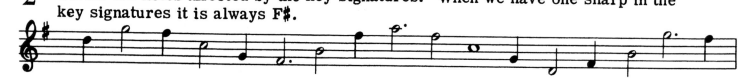

When we have one flat in the key signature it is always B♭.

3 On what count do the following examples start?

LESSON 20

1 a - Write 2 B♭'s and give
   fingering.

b - Write 2 F♯'s and give
   fingering.

c - Write 2 C♯'s and give fingering.

d - Write 2 G♯'s and give fingering.

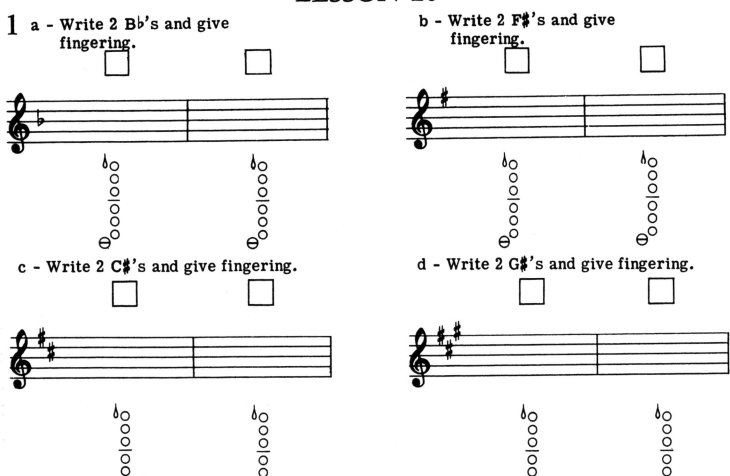

2 Circle the notes affected by the key signatures. When we have 2 sharps they are always
   F♯ & C♯.

When we have 3 sharps they are F♯, C♯, & G♯.

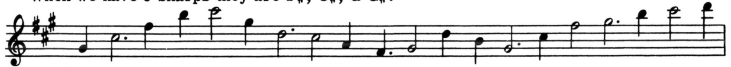

3 Add notes or rests to the measures below so each measure contains the correct number of counts.

24

LESSON 21

Eighth Notes

We have had drill using 4 kinds of notes and rests.

o - whole note; [whole rest] - whole rest; = 4 counts

𝅘𝅥. - dotted half note; - - - - - - - - - - - = 3 counts

𝅗𝅥 = half note; [half rest] - half rest; = 2 counts

𝅘𝅥 - quarter note; **𝄽** - quarter rest; = 1 count

From now on our work will include eighth notes. The eighth note gets only one half count and it takes two of them to make one count. In other words, two eighth notes are played on one count.

A single eighth note looks like this - 𝅘𝅥𝅮
When we have two together on one
count they are joined like this - 𝅘𝅥𝅮𝅘𝅥𝅮
This is an eighth rest - 𝄾

1 In the measures below, on what count do we play the eighth notes?

___ ___ ___ ___ & ___ ___ & ___

2 Put in the Bars and write counts.

3 a - Complete the Time signature.
b - Write counting under each measure.

E.L. 451

LESSON 22

1   a - Name the notes.
       b - Mark fingering.

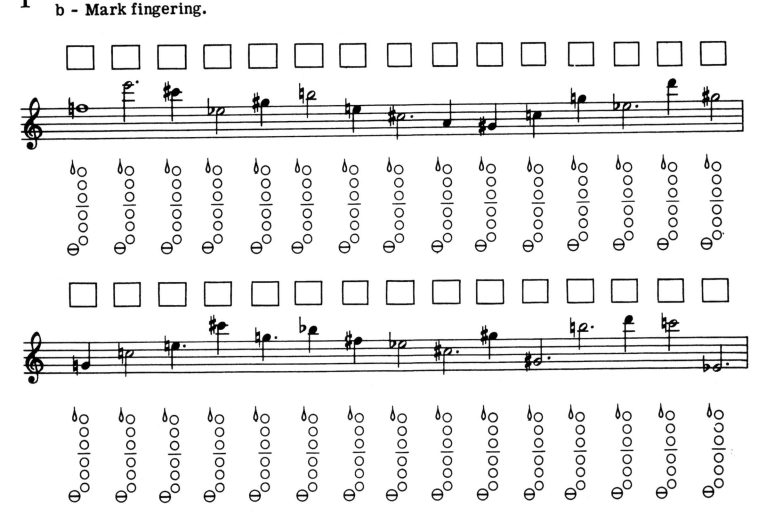

2   Sometimes we have different names for the same tone. For instance E♭ and D♯ are the same tone. These notes are called Enharmonic Tones. The following rule applies in most cases (except between B & C; E & F).

         One note sharped is the same as the noted above flatted.
         One note flatted is the same as the note below sharped.

On the staff below write another note that is the same as the given note.

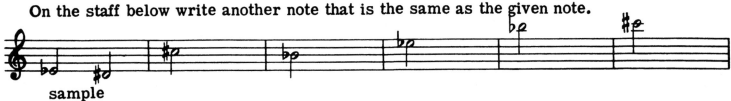

sample

E.L. 451

LESSON 23

1 Join the stems on the notes below so you have the correct number of counts in each measure. The first measure is done for you.

Sample

2 a - Complete the measures below with either notes or rests. (Note Time signature).

3 a - Put in Measure bars. (Note Time signature).
   b - Write counting under each measure.

LESSON 24

1 a - Give two ways to finger each of the notes below.
b - Name the notes. (See fingering chart (page 3) when necessary.

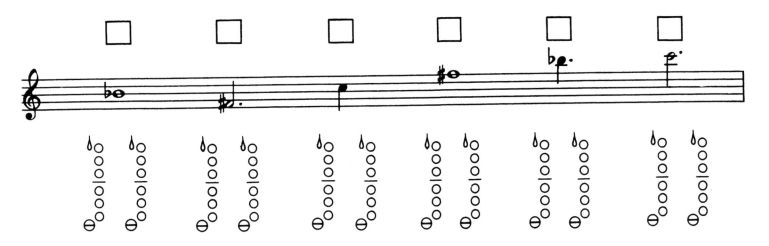

2 Circle the notes affected by the key signatures.

3 Write counting under each measure.

LESSON 25

1 Make each note either one half step higher or lower as indicated. H means higher; L means lower. <u>Warning</u> - Be sure you take the Key signature into consideration. The first one is a sample.

H   L   L   L   H   L   H   L   L   L   H

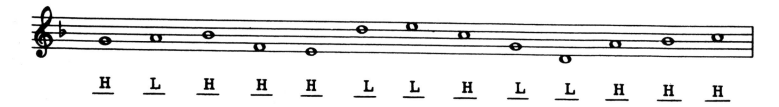

H   L   H   H   H   L   L   H   L   L   H   H   H

2   a - Write the notes below one Octave lower.

etc.

b - Write the notes below one Octave higher.

etc.

LESSON 26
A Camping Trip

In this story the missing words are spelled in notes. Fill in the blanks and you will have the complete story.

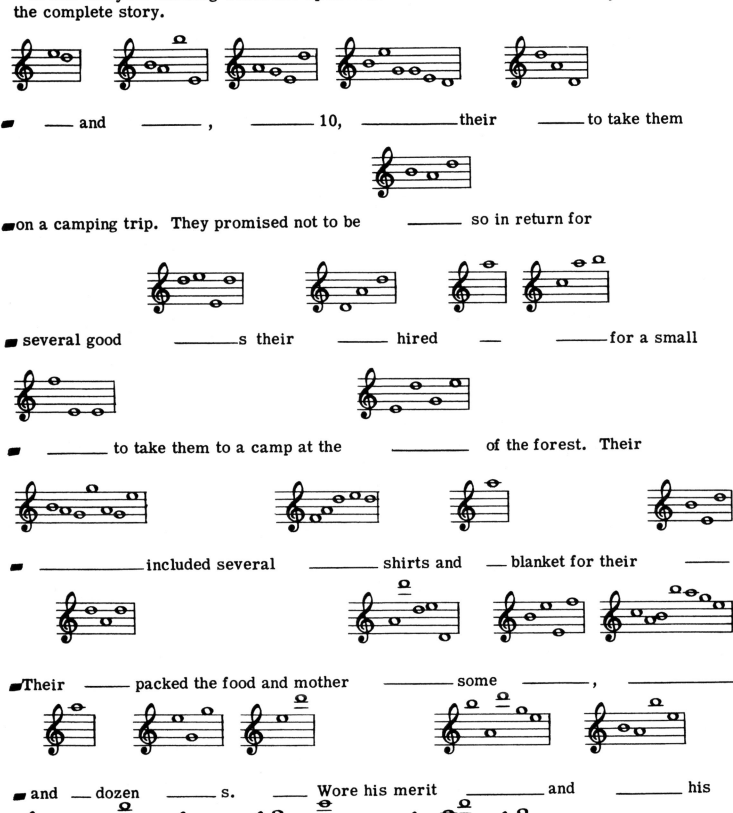

___ — and _____ , _____ 10, _____ their _____ to take them

on a camping trip. They promised not to be _____ so in return for

several good _____s their _____ hired — _____for a small

_____ to take them to a camp at the _____ of the forest. Their

_____included several _____ shirts and — blanket for their _____

Their _____ packed the food and mother _____ some _____, _____

and — dozen _____s. ___ Wore his merit _____ and _____ his

_____belt. ___, _____ and their _____ _____goodbye to mother

and were off.

Speed Test Number 1

Name the notes. Work for speed. Each test should be completed in
1 min. and 30 seconds or less.

Time _____ Seconds

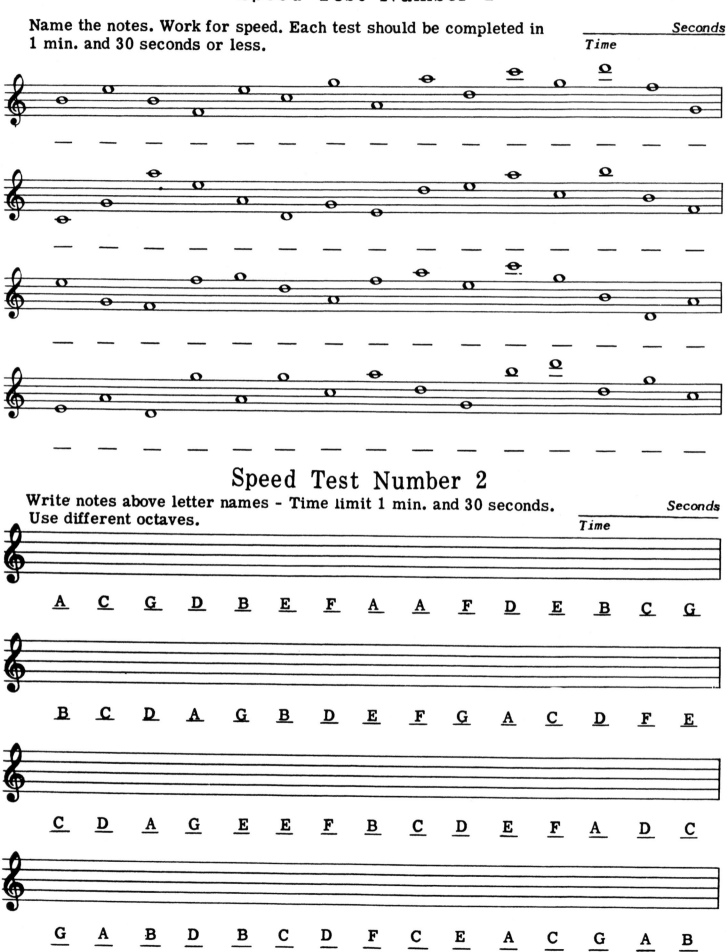

Speed Test Number 2

Write notes above letter names - Time limit 1 min. and 30 seconds.
Use different octaves.

Time _____ Seconds

A   C   G   D   B   E   F   A   A   F   D   E   B   C   G

B   C   D   A   G   B   D   E   F   G   A   C   D   F   E

C   D   A   G   E   E   F   B   C   D   E   F   A   D   C

G   A   B   D   B   C   D   F   C   E   A   C   G   A   B

Speed Test Number 3

Name notes - Time limit - 1 min. and 30 seconds.

Speed Test Number 4

Write the notes above the letter names - Time limit 1 min. and 30 seconds. Use different octaves.

A   C   D   F   A   E   C   B   G   B   A   C   D   E   F

G   D   C   B   A   C   E   A   F   G   E   B   D   F   G

C   D   F   G   A   C   B   D   E   B   F   A   G   B   E

D   C   A   F   A   G   B   C   F   E   C   E   B   D   G

E.L. 451

Glossary

1. ≣ staff.

2. 𝄞 - treble clef sign.

3. 𝄢 - bass clef sign.

4. 4/4 - time signature.

5. ≣ bar.

6. ≣ double bar.

7. ≣ measure.

8. ♭ - flat - lowers a note a 1/2 step.

9. ♯ - sharp - raises a note 1/2 step.

10. ♮ - natural - cancels a sharp or flat.

11. ≣ leger lines.

12. ≣ tie.

13. ≣ slur.

14. C - common time. (Same as 4/4 time)

15. 𝄆 repeat section between two sets of dots.

16. D.C. - Da Capo - go back to beginning.

17. D.S. - Del Segna - go back to sign (𝄋).

18. Fine - finish - the end.

19. ⌒ - hold or fermata - give extra time.

20. ⁒ - repeat preceding measure.

21. 1st and 2nd endings. Play 1st ending the first time - then repeat strain and play 2nd ending the second time.

22. ⊕ - coda sign - go to coda.

23. 𝄋 - sign.

24. Key Signature - Flats or sharps placed at the beginning of each line to indicate certain notes that are to be sharped or flatted.

25. *pp* - pianissimo - very soft.

26. *p* - piano - soft.

27. *mp* - mezzo piano - moderately soft.

28. *mf* - mezzo forte - moderately loud.

29. *f* - forte - loud.

30. *ff* - fortissimo - very loud.

31. < - increase volume.

32. > - decrease volume.

33. rit. - ritard - gradually slower.

34. rall. - rallentando - gradually slower.

35. accel. - accelerando - gradually faster.

36. cresc. - crescendo - gradually louder.

37. dim. - diminuendo - gradually softer.

38. Chromatic scale - a scale that progresses by half steps.

39. ¢ - alla breve, or cut time.

40. > - accent mark - play with force.

41. simile - continue in similar manner.

42. ♪ - staccato - short and repeated.

43. ♪♪♪ - triplets - three notes played in the time of two.